Hueber Lektüren

Lucky for Some

Paula Smith

Illustrated by Paul Könye

Hueber Verlag

This is the German version of **Lucky for Some**

Lucky for Some

ILTS Created and developed by
International Language Teaching Services Ltd
Business and Technology Centre, Shire Hill
Saffron Walden, Essex CB11 3AQ, UK

help@ilts.info
www.ilts.info

Author: Paula Smith
Series editor: James Bean
Illustrations: Paul Könye
Text design: ILTS Ltd
Origination: Prepress-Solutions.com

3. 2. 1. Die letzten Ziffern
2013 12 11 10 09 bezeichnen Zahl und Jahr des Druckes.
Alle Drucke dieser Auflage können, da unverändert, nebeneinander benutzt werden.
1. Auflage

Redaktion: Heike Birner, Hueber Verlag, Ismaning
Umschlaggestaltung: Parzhuber & Partner, München
Umschlagfoto: © getty images/Digital Vision
Druck und Bindung: Ludwig Auer GmbH, Donauwörth
Printed in Germany
ISBN 978–3–19–322976–2 (Package)
33.2976 (Buch)

Contents

Chapter 1

A new team

Madison Munroe sat at the kitchen table and put butter on her toast. Her twin brother Daniel walked in, smiled at her and said, 'Hi. Is it your first training session today?'

'Yes,' sighed Madison. 'My first session with the Colby Raiders.'

'How are you feeling?' asked Daniel.

Madison sighed again and put down her knife. 'Okay, I think. It's hard to join a new team. I loved my old team.'

'Oh, you always make friends easily,' he said.

'Well, I used to think that,' she said slowly, 'but now...'

'What's wrong?' Daniel asked. 'Is school okay?'

Madison shrugged her shoulders and smiled at her brother. 'Yes, it's okay. It's just hard to start at a new school. And I don't like being at an all-girls school – I miss going to school with you!' She finished her toast and stood up. 'I must go. I don't want to be late.'

'Good luck at the training session,' said Daniel.

Madison opened the gate and stepped onto the street. She turned to close the gate and looked up at the house.

It's a nice house, she thought. *And Colby is a nice town. I am going to like it one day. I have to!*

But it was hard. Madison loved her old town, her old school and her old friends.

I have to stop thinking about the old things, she thought. *I don't want Mum and Dad to see me feeling sad. They have a lot to worry about. They didn't want to move here.*

After school that afternoon Madison pushed open the door

of the Colby Sports Centre and went inside. She was early. She went to the changing rooms and got ready. Then she came out and picked up a basketball. She bounced it around the court. She threw it into the hoop and smiled to herself.

Now I feel better, she thought. *Basketball always makes me feel better.* She threw the ball into the hoop again.

Some girls came in, all in white jerseys.

My new team, thought Madison. *The Colby Raiders A Team. Will they like me?*

Then a tall man came in and said, 'Okay, girls! Come over here, please.'

That's Mr Roberts, the coach, thought Madison.

He saw Madison and asked, 'Are you Madison Munroe?'

Madison nodded and tried to smile at everyone.

'Okay, girls! This is your new teammate, Madison,' said Mr Roberts. 'She's just moved here. She used to play for the Jesmond Jets. I've spoken to their coach about her. She was their best player! We're lucky to have her.'

Madison felt her face go red. *Oh great,* she thought. *Now they're* really *going to love me!*

The coach gave her a white jersey with the number nine on it. 'Quickly go and put that on and then we can start.'

Madison ran to the changing rooms and put the jersey on. She felt her stomach turn. *Oh, stop it, Madison!* she said to herself. *You don't usually get nervous.*

She walked out and saw the girls look at her jersey. One of the girls said something quietly to another girl. The two of them smiled at each other, and it wasn't a friendly smile.

What's wrong with them? thought Madison. Then she told herself, *Remember – you were the Jesmond Jets' best player. Okay, here we go.*

And she ran onto the basketball court.

EXIT

An hour later she walked unhappily back to the changing rooms with the other girls and got changed.

I played really badly, she thought. *What was wrong with me?*

The girl next to her smiled and said, 'Hi, I'm Bella, and this is my friend Christine.'

Madison smiled at them. 'Hi. Have you played in the team for long?'

'This is our second year,' said Christine. 'Some girls have played in the team for three or four years.'

Madison looked across at the other girls. *They've all played together for a long time*, she thought. *Now they have a new teammate, and she isn't very good*.

'I played really badly,' she said to Bella and Christine.

'Don't worry,' Bella said kindly. 'It's hard to join a new team in the middle of the year.'

Just then some of the girls walked past them. 'Maybe it's the number nine jersey working its magic again,' said one girl nastily. Her friends laughed and they left the room.

'Oh, don't worry about Eva,' said Christine. 'She likes to be the best player. She's Coach Roberts's daughter.'

'Yes, and she always likes to tell us that!' said Bella.

'But what did she say about the number nine jersey?' asked Madison. 'It's working its magic? What magic?'

'Oh, don't listen to those stories,' said Bella.

'What stories?' asked Madison.

Bella looked at Christine, and Christine looked at Bella. Then Bella said quietly, 'Well, a girl from this school disappeared. She played in this team.'

'She disappeared?' asked Madison.

'It was a long time ago,' said Bella.

'But what happened to her?'

'Well, the story isn't very nice,' said Christine. 'It was a murder.'

'Someone killed her?' asked Madison. 'Is that true?'

'No, Christine,' said Bella. 'It wasn't a murder. Someone kidnapped her and then no one saw her ever again.'

Madison looked at Bella and then at Christine. 'But which story is true?' she asked.

'Well, I don't know,' said Christine. 'It was a long time ago. I only heard a story about it.'

'But...what has this got to do with me?' asked Madison.

'It's the jersey,' said Bella. 'You see, she wore the number nine jersey. And since that time, unlucky things have happened to every player in the number nine jersey.'

'What kind of things?'

'Well, two years ago, Pauline had to stop playing basketball. She got very bad asthma,' said Christine. 'And the girl before her fell off her bike and broke her arm.'

'And then there was the girl who had a car accident,' said Bella. 'And last year there was Claire.'

'Goodness, what happened to Claire?' asked Madison.

'Well, nothing really bad,' said Bella, 'but she had lots of little things go wrong. Things disappeared from her school locker. And just before the big match of the year, she broke her finger.'

'But that's just bad luck. Anyone can have bad luck,' said Madison.

'The coach always gives out the number nine jersey last,' said Christine. 'That's because it's unlucky.'

'I'm not superstitious,' said Madison. 'I'm happy to wear the number nine jersey.'

'Well,' said Bella slowly, 'you didn't play very well today. But you were the best player in your old team, weren't you? Isn't that a bit strange?'

'Not really,' said Madison. 'It's just hard to join a new team.' She picked up her bag and smiled at the girls. 'I think number nine is going to be lucky for me,' she said, and left the room.

Chapter 2

The coach's office

But Madison didn't start to play better. The Colby Raiders played games against other teams. They won some and they lost some, but Madison played badly in all of them.

After another bad game one Saturday, she sat down on the seats beside Bella and Christine. She felt sad and angry.

'Are you okay?' Bella asked.

'Oh, I don't know. I used to be a good player, but something's wrong with me,' Madison said. 'We lost the game today because I played badly.'

'Oh, that's not true, Madison,' said Bella kindly. 'And even the best sports people play badly sometimes.'

The other girls in the team walked past to go to the changing rooms. They glared at Madison.

'Loser!' said Eva quietly.

Madison groaned.

'Oh, don't worry about them,' said Christine. 'Eva is nasty to everyone. And the others just follow her.'

'Yes, I know,' said Madison. 'I just want to play better.'

Just then the door opened and one of her teammates called to her, 'Madison, the coach wants to see you in his office after you've changed.'

'Oh, great,' groaned Madison. 'This is not going to be good.'

Ten minutes later she came out of the changing rooms. Mr Roberts walked past and said, 'Madison, can you wait in my office, please? I'll be there soon.'

Madison nodded and went into the coach's office.

She looked around her. She felt nervous.

The coach isn't happy with me, she thought.

She walked over to a bookshelf and looked at the large books there. Carefully she took one off the shelf. She looked inside the book.

Wow, she thought. *These are the log books from each year. This one's from 1985*. She saw the names of all the players in the team. She put the book back and looked at all the others on the shelf. *They go back to 1975.*

She turned around and looked at the walls. There were photographs of all the teams. The first one was from 1975 too.

This team started more than thirty years ago, she thought.

She looked at all the teams from all the years. In each one, she looked at the girl in the number nine jersey.

Just then the coach came back into the room. 'Ah, yes, Madison,' he said. 'I need to talk with you. How do you feel you are doing?'

'Oh, it's a great team,' Madison said quickly. 'I really like playing with the girls.'

'Yes, yes,' said the coach. 'But the thing is, you're not playing well.'

Madison nodded her head. *Oh no*, she thought. *What is he going to do? Okay Madison, stay calm. Don't cry! Please don't cry!*

'The coach from your old team told me good things about you. He said to me, "Madison's a great player. She's my best player." But was that true, Madison?'

'Oh, yes, Coach, it was true. I am a good player. Well, I *was* a good player...in the Jets.'

'Madison, you're not in the Jets now. You're in a new team,' the coach replied, 'and the Colby Raiders need you to play well!'

He's angry with me, thought Madison. *I am trying to play well.* She felt her face go red. She tried to stay calm. She didn't speak.

The coach said, 'I've decided to give you two weeks. Two more games. I want to see you play better in that time,' he said, 'or you'll be playing in the B Team.'

Madison felt her face go white. *The B Team! I don't want to play in the B Team. I have to play better. I have to work harder.*

'I'm sorry, Mr Roberts,' she said. 'I have been playing badly. That's true, but I...I am a good player. I'll train harder. I'll play better. You'll see.'

'Well, you can start with our next game,' he said, and waited for her to leave.

Then Madison thought of something. She looked at the photos on the wall. 'Coach,' she said, 'the girls told me about the number nine jersey. What happened to that girl all those years ago?'

'What are you saying, Madison?' the coach said angrily. 'You're playing badly because of your jersey?'

'No, I just wondered –' said Madison.

'Well, don't,' said the coach. 'There's nothing wrong with the number nine. That's just a silly superstition.'

'I'm not superstitious,' said Madison. 'I just wondered about the girl.'

The coach looked at one of the photos on the wall – the one from 1979. He was quiet for a moment. Madison waited.

'It was a long time ago,' he said slowly. 'A long time before I became the coach. Something happened to one of the girls. But I don't know what.' Then he walked over to his desk and sat down. He didn't look up.

Madison thanked him quietly and left the room.

Wow, that was strange, she thought. *Maybe he does know something. But what is it?*

She walked home slowly, and thought about her talk with the coach.

Chapter 3

A girl doesn't just disappear

Madison opened the front door, dropped her bag in the hall and walked into the kitchen.

She opened the fridge door. She wanted something to eat. She wanted to feel better.

Daniel walked into the room, sat down at the kitchen table and opened his schoolbooks. 'How did the training go?' he asked.

'Don't ask!' said Madison. She took a large piece of cake from a box and sat down at the table. She picked up a fork, glared at the cake and then dug the fork into it.

'Ouch!' said Daniel, and laughed. 'That poor cake!'

Madison looked up and glared at him. She held her fork up.

'Hey, what's wrong?' Daniel asked.

Madison shrugged her shoulders and put down her fork. She tried to smile but she wanted to cry. 'I just had to go and see the coach. He's not happy with me.'

'Why not?' asked Daniel.

'Because I'm not playing well,' she said sadly.

'But you've just moved here. It's a new team. You need time,' said Daniel angrily.

'Yes, I know. But he's right. Something's wrong with me. I am playing badly. And now I only have two weeks to play better. After that, he's going to put me in the B Team. I don't want to go down to the B Team.'

She glared at the cake again and then pushed the plate towards her brother. 'This is not helping,' she said. 'Do you want it?'

Daniel took the plate and smiled at his sister. He picked up the fork and gently took a piece of cake. He put it in his mouth and closed his eyes. 'Mmm,' he said. 'Now this is the way to eat a piece of cake!'

Madison laughed.

Daniel smiled and said, 'You're a very good player, Madison. You know that.'

'*Was* a good player,' said Madison. 'But maybe those stories are right.'

'What stories?' asked Daniel.

Madison told him about the number nine jersey. She told him about the girl.

'And what happened to her?' asked Daniel.

'I don't know,' she said. 'Christine and Bella didn't know. There are stories about it. No one ever saw her again…maybe it was a murder. I asked the coach about her, and he got angry with me. But it was strange. He stared at a team photo on the wall – the one from 1979. Maybe he does know something.'

'That *is* strange,' said Daniel. He was quiet for a moment and then he said, 'A girl doesn't just disappear, Madison. *Something* happened to her. Do you want to find out?'

'Well, I am curious, but I don't know. How can we find out?' she asked. 'I don't know the girl's name.'

'That's easy,' said Daniel. 'We just have to look at the photo on the office wall.'

'Oh, I don't want to go back in there,' said Madison. 'The coach won't like –'

'Are you scared?' asked Daniel.

'No, of course I'm not,' said Madison. 'I'm not scared of the coach, but I want to play in the A Team. I don't want him to get angry with me.'

'Okay, but maybe I can look at the photograph,' said Daniel. 'I can come to the next training session. I can look in the office and try to find out the name of the girl.'

'Oh, Daniel, I don't know...'

'I want to come. When is it?'

'It's on Monday afternoon. But –'

'I'll be there. I want to see you play – to cheer you on!'

'Okay. Thanks, Daniel,' said Madison.

At the training session on Monday, Madison felt nervous. She looked over to the seats. Daniel waved at her. She smiled and waved back at him. Then the game started and she forgot about him. Ten minutes later she looked back at the seats and he wasn't there.

Be careful, Daniel, she thought. *I don't want any trouble.*

Daniel waited until the coach was busy talking to the girls. He walked away from the basketball court and stood at the door to the office. He looked around him and then opened the door and went in.

He looked at the pictures on the wall. *Where's the photo for 1979? Ah, here it is. And there's number nine. She's pretty. Oh, good – there's a list of names under the picture. Okay, she's the third girl from the left. Now, where's the third name? Here it is: Maxine Lucas. That's her. That's the girl.*

Daniel walked to the door and listened. He heard the coach shouting at the girls.

He went back in and looked at the books on the bookshelf. He found the log book for 1979 and took it off the shelf. Someone had written about every training session and every game. He looked through the pages. Then he found it.

'...training session very quiet today. No one has seen Maxine Lucas for three days. No word on her yet...'

Daniel looked at the date on the page. Then he put the book back on the shelf and quietly left the office. He walked back to sit and wait for Madison.

Daniel told her about the name and the log book on the way home.

'What do we do next?' asked Madison.

'Let's start at the library,' said Daniel. 'They have all the old newspapers. We can meet there after school tomorrow.'

Chapter 4

Finding Maxine Lucas

Madison went to the library after school on Tuesday. Daniel was already there. They asked about the old newspapers. But the librarian couldn't help. The library didn't have newspapers from 1979.

They went home and went onto the Internet. They looked for information about Maxine Lucas. There were pages and pages about people with that name, but they didn't see any information about a Maxine Lucas from Colby.

'It will take months to go through all these,' sighed Madison.

'Yes, it isn't much help. Maybe we need to try something else,' said Daniel.

'Maybe we need to give up and *do* something else,' said Madison. 'I have to do some basketball practice today. It's a big game for me on Saturday.'

Daniel looked at the computer screen, and then said, 'What about the phone book? We can find the Lucases from Colby in there.'

'And then what?' asked Madison.

'We call them!' answered Daniel.

'Oh, Daniel, we can't,' said Madison. 'We don't know them.'

'Okay, you don't want to? Well, you can play basketball,' said Daniel. 'But I'm going to look in the phone book.'

He got up and went out of the room. A minute later he came back in with the phone book. He sat down and found the right page. 'Here we are – Lucas. Hmm…There are about thirty people here. That's not bad. We can call thirty people. What do you think?'

Madison looked at her brother and sighed. 'Well, okay.'

'Good!' said Daniel.

'But what do we say to them?'

Daniel picked up a piece of paper and a pencil. 'We're doing a project for school. A history project – on the history of our town. The project has to be on something from thirty years ago. And we've decided to find out about Maxine Lucas. What happened to her?'

'But maybe it *was* a murder, Daniel. We can't ask questions about that. People won't want to talk about it.'

'We have to try, Madison, or we'll never find out.'

'Well, I'm not sure...' said Madison. 'You do the talking.'

'Okay, give me the phone,' said Daniel. 'I'll call the first one.'

He called the number and they waited. Then he spoke. 'Hello. My name's Daniel Munroe. You don't know me, but I'm doing a school project on the history of our town. I'm calling you because I want to find out about someone called Maxine Lucas. You see, your name's Lucas – Well, you know *that*, of course, but I wondered – Do you – or did you ever – know anyone with that name?...It's Maxine. Maxine Lucas...You don't?' Daniel looked at Madison and shook his head. 'Oh, well, I'm sorry to bother you, sir. Thank you...goodbye.'

He put down the phone and said, 'No luck. He doesn't know anyone called Maxine Lucas. But that wasn't hard, was it? You try the next one.'

'Okay,' said Madison, and she called the next number.

Twenty-five minutes later she said, 'Well, no luck yet. We've spoken to seven people and no one knows a Maxine Lucas. Let's stop for today. I need a break and Mum will be home soon. I don't want her to know about this. Do you want something to drink?'

'Yes, please. Then I'll come out and play basketball with you. I need some fresh air.'

'Okay. We can call some more people tomorrow after school,' said Madison.

On Wednesday afternoon they sat down to call some more people.

'No luck with the first seven yesterday,' said Daniel. 'Maybe today someone will know Maxine Lucas.'

They took it in turns to call people on the list. Madison went first and then Daniel did the next one. He started to talk to someone and then waved across the table at Madison. 'You *do* know a Maxine Lucas?' he asked. 'She played basketball here in the 1970s...She's your second cousin? Oh, that's great.' He held his thumb up to his sister. 'Yes, sir...No, I understand. You don't want to give us her number...No, we don't want to upset her. We...we just want to talk to her about – about those times.'

Madison was on her feet in front of Daniel. 'What's he saying?' she whispered. 'Is he going to let us talk to her?'

Daniel held his finger up to his lips. 'Yes, sir, that's a good idea. I'll give you my number and you can call us back. It's 925 3501...Yes, that's right. Well, thank you very much, Mr Lucas. I look forward to hearing from you. Thank you.'

He put the phone down and smiled at Madison. 'Okay, okay, calm down,' he said. 'Maxine Lucas is alive and well, but she doesn't live in this town any more. He's her second cousin. He'll talk to her and tell her about us.'

'When is he going to ask her? When is he going to call us back?' asked Madison.

'In a few days,' said Daniel.

Madison nodded and smiled. She looked at the list of names again and said, 'We were lucky –' Then she said, ' Oh!'

'What is it?' asked Daniel.

'Oh, nothing. It's just that he's number nine on the list!' said Madison.

'Ooh! Spooky number nine!' said Daniel.

Madison laughed and threw her cushion at Daniel's head.

On Friday evening Madison and Daniel were in the kitchen.

'How are you feeling about your big game tomorrow?' asked Daniel.

'Nervous,' said Madison. 'I just have to start playing better. But I –'

Just then the phone rang. Daniel answered it and then waved a hand at Madison. 'Mr Lucas! Thank you for calling back,' he said.

Madison went and stood beside Daniel.

'You've talked to her? Oh, that's good,' he said, and nodded at Madison. 'Yes, we'll be very happy to meet her...Yes, of course...Oh, I see...Yes, I understand. Oh, I'll just get a pen and paper.'

Madison passed him some paper and a pen and whispered, 'What's he saying?'

Daniel wrote something on the paper. 'Thank you very much, Mr Lucas. That's great...No, I understand. We are really looking forward to meeting her. Please tell her that...Thank you. Goodbye.'

Daniel put the phone down.

'Well?' asked Madison. 'What did he say?'

'She's going to meet us,' said Daniel. 'Next week, on Wednesday at 4 pm, at Mimo's Café in the Mall.'

'That's great,' said Madison.

'She doesn't often come back here,' said Daniel. 'But she'll be in town next Wednesday, and she'll meet us then.'

Chapter 5

The meeting

The next Wednesday they stood outside the café.

'Okay, are you ready?' asked Daniel.

'Well, yes,' said Madison. 'But Daniel, we aren't doing a school project. We'll have to tell her that. Will she be angry with us?'

'I don't know,' said Daniel, 'but there's only one way to find out.' He pushed open the door.

They walked into the café and looked around.

'Look, over in the corner. Is that her?' asked Madison.

Daniel looked over to the table in the corner. A woman sat there with a cup of coffee. 'Yes,' he said, 'I remember her face from the photo.'

She looked up and saw them. They smiled at her and she waved back.

'Hello,' she said. 'Are you Madison and Daniel?'

'Yes, we are,' the two of them said together.

'I'm Maxine Lucas. Please come and sit down.'

Madison and Daniel sat down at the table. The waitress came over and the two of them ordered hot chocolates.

'So, you're working on a school project?' asked Maxine Lucas.

'Umm, well not really,' said Madison quickly.

'Oh? But Michael said –'

'It's not a project, but we want to ask you some questions,' said Daniel.

'Questions?' said Maxine.

'We've just moved to Colby, and I've joined a basketball team,' said Madison. 'The Colby Raiders.'

'Oh, really? I used to play for the Raiders,' said Maxine.

'I know. I wear the number nine jersey,' said Madison.

'Oh! That was my jersey!' said Maxine. 'But I don't understand. Why do you want to talk to me?'

'Well...' Madison didn't know where to start. 'I used to be a very good player. But then I joined the Raiders, and I've been playing really badly. The coach isn't happy with me. I have to play better or I'll be out of the team.'

'But how can I help you with that?' asked Maxine.

'Madison is having a hard time in the team,' said Daniel. 'Some of the girls aren't very friendly and they talk behind Madison's back. There are stories about the number nine jersey. It's unlucky – or, that's what people say.'

'The number nine jersey is unlucky? Why?' asked Maxine.

'Well,' said Madison, 'because a girl disappeared in 1979. Something happened to her...Maybe it was a murd–'

She stopped. She suddenly felt very silly.

Daniel helped his sister. 'It was you, Maxine. We want to ask you about 1979. What happened to you?'

Maxine was quiet for a moment. Then she said, 'I didn't disappear. I ran away...' She stopped, and Madison saw tears in her eyes. Maxine took a deep breath and carried on. 'I ran away from home. At the time I was very unhappy. My parents wanted to get a divorce. And then at basketball one of the girls was very nasty to me. It was really bad. That made me more unhappy. But I didn't tell my parents. I felt very alone. So I ran away. But it wasn't easy. I had nowhere to go...' Maxine stopped again. This time tears fell from her eyes.

'I'm sorry. I didn't want to upset you,' said Madison gently.

'What happened?' asked Daniel.

'I lived on the street. Well, I slept down by the river. There was a group of us, all young people. We took care of each other.'

'Wasn't that very hard?' said Madison. She thought about her warm bed.

'It was horrible. Horrible. I was scared all of the time. It was very cold and there were bad people around too,' said Maxine.

'How long did you live there?' asked Madison.

'For three months,' said Maxine. 'Then one night there was a bad fight. I was very scared. And that was it. I didn't want to be there another minute. The next morning I got up and left. I went to find my aunt. She was pleased to see me. I don't think I ever really thought about my parents. I hurt them very badly.'

Madison said, 'I'm sorry. You don't have to talk about this.' She wanted to cry too.

'No, no, it's okay. It's good to talk about it,' said Maxine. 'I stayed with my aunt for a while. Then my mother decided to move out of Colby. There was a lot of talk – a lot of gossip. She found a new place to live, and I went to live with her. I went to a new school. We started a new life. It was better, much better. The only mistake I made was giving up basketball. At the time I didn't want to play any more and I never wanted to see Anita, the nasty girl, again. But I loved playing basketball. It was silly to give it up.'

'I love it too,' said Madison.

The waitress brought Madison and Daniel's hot chocolates. The three of them sat and drank without speaking. Madison thought about Maxine's story. It was sad.

Then Maxine asked, 'Are the Raiders still a good team?'

'Oh, yes, they have some great players,' said Madison. 'Eva is very good. But she doesn't like me. She's nasty to me.'

'What does the coach do about it?' asked Maxine. 'Have you told him?'

'No, I haven't. She's his daughter, you see. I don't think he likes me very much anyway!'

Daniel said, 'There's a picture of the team in this week's *Colby News*.' He went to a table near the front of the café and picked up a newspaper. He opened the paper and looked for the story. 'They played a big game on Saturday.'

'Oh, Daniel, don't talk about that,' said Madison. 'I played badly again.'

'Yes, here it is,' said Daniel, and he showed the newspaper story to Maxine.

She read the article and then looked at the picture of the team. In the corner was a smaller picture of the coach with his daughter Eva and his wife. Maxine's face went white.

'What's wrong, Maxine?' asked Daniel. 'Are you okay?'

'That's her! That's Anita!' She pointed to the picture of the coach's wife. 'She's older of course, but that's her.' She looked at the names under the picture. 'Yes – Anita. And that's Jack Roberts. I know him. He used to play in the boys' team. He was the captain. Well, well, they got married! And now they have a daughter and she is bullying you.' Maxine shook her head.

'Oh, she's just unfriendly. She doesn't say much to me – just the thing about the jersey, really.'

'Well, there's nothing wrong with the number nine jersey,' said Maxine. 'I loved my jersey. I played well. And you can too.'

They finished their drinks and got up to pay.

'Thank you for meeting us,' said Madison. 'I didn't want to upset you. I was curious, but I didn't really think about you and...and your story. I'm sorry.'

Maxine put her hand on Madison's arm. 'No. Thank *you*. It's been good to talk to you. I never really talked about it with my mother. She didn't like to. I'm glad to have met you. Please don't feel bad.'

'Well, there's nothing wrong with the number nine jersey. We know that now,' said Daniel.

'Of course there isn't,' said Maxine. 'You play your best and be sure to stand up to Eva. That's the only way to stop her. Don't make my mistake. I needed to stand up to Anita...' She stopped and thought for a moment. '...I *need* to stand up to Anita.'

She gave Madison a hug and left.

Chapter 6

Lucky number nine

On Saturday morning Madison sat on her bed to put on her basketball shoes. She felt sick.

Daniel put his head around her door and said, 'Hi. Are you ready for the game?'

'No,' said Madison. 'I feel sick.'

'Well, be sick on Eva's shoes,' laughed Daniel. 'Come on, we're leaving in ten minutes.'

'That's a big help. Thanks,' said Madison.

She left her parents and Daniel in the car park and went to get ready. The office door was open. The coach was in there, and his wife was there too. He was angry. Another person was in there, but Madison couldn't see who it was. She walked past the office and looked back. Then she stopped. Maxine Lucas was in the office with the coach! Madison quickly looked again. Maxine was talking calmly.

Madison put her head down and walked quickly to the changing rooms. She didn't want them to see her. *What is Maxine doing here?* she thought. *Why is the coach angry? Please don't tell him about our meeting, Maxine, or I'll be in the B Team for sure!*

She wanted to stay in the changing room. But she had to play this game. And she had to play well.

She sighed and walked out of the changing room with her head up high. She went to the corner of the basketball court, where her teammates were getting ready.

'I wonder...will the number nine jersey bring you bad luck today?' said Eva nastily.

Madison turned and looked at her. She remembered Maxine's words: *...be sure to stand up to Eva. That's the only way to stop her.*

'Of course it won't,' she said. 'It *can't*, Eva. It's just a jersey.' She turned away, and she heard Bella and Christine laugh.

Wow! Maxine was right, she thought. *It feels good to stand up to her*. She smiled at Bella and Christine.

Then the coach came over to them. 'Okay, everyone,' he said. 'This is a big game today, and we need to win this one. I want everyone to play their best.'

The girls all nodded.

Well, he isn't too *angry*, thought Madison.

The girls walked away, but the coach called her. 'Madison, wait a minute, please.'

This is it, she thought. *He's going to ask me to leave.*

'Yes, Coach?' she said.

Coach Roberts looked at her for a moment. He opened his mouth to say something. Then he stopped. He looked at her again and said, 'Good luck today.' Then he gave her a note. Madison took it. Her hand shook. She looked at the coach, but he didn't look at her. He just walked away.

Madison opened the note and read it:

I loved wearing the number nine jersey. It's lucky for some. Show them your best, and thank you.

Your friend, Maxine

Madison ran onto the court and looked up at the seats. She saw Daniel and her mother and father. Then she saw Maxine come and sit next to Daniel. Maxine waved at Madison. Then she held up her thumbs. Madison smiled and waved back.

15
9
32
12

She stood on the court and waited for the whistle to blow. She looked down and touched her jersey.

'Come on, number nine,' she said. 'Lucky for some! Lucky for me!'

The whistle blew. The game was on!

Activities

Chapter 1

Before you read

A. Look at the picture on page 5 and circle the correct answers.

1. Where are these people?
   a. in a classroom b. in a kitchen c. in a café
2. What are they doing?
   a. talking b. cooking c. reading

B. Find these words in your dictionary. Use them in the sentences.

toast join usually disappeared

1. Have you seen a little brown dog? He was sitting there a minute ago but now he has ____disappeared____.
2. Luke ____usually____ gets to school early but today he is late.
3. Brad wants to ____join____ the army when he leaves school.
4. Millie has tea and ____toast____ for breakfast every day.

C. Listen to Track 3 on the CD and answer these questions.

1. Who was joining a new team?
   a. Madison b. Daniel
2. What kind of school was Madison's new school?
   a. an all-girls school b. an all-boys school
3. Who was Daniel?
   a. Madison's father b. Madison's brother

After you read

Comprehension

A. Circle the correct answers.

1. When did Madison go to the Colby Sports Centre?
   a. in the morning b. in the afternoon c. in the evening
2. What sport did she play with the Colby Raiders?
   a. basketball b. baseball c. netball
3. Where did she go to get ready?
   a. to her school b. to the changing rooms
   c. to the basketball court
4. What colour jerseys did the Colby Raiders wear?
   a. black b. blue c. white

B. Circle T for true or F for false for these sentences.

1. Madison and Daniel were twins. T / F
2. Madison hated her old team. T / F
3. Madison missed going to school with Daniel. T / F
4. Madison played well at the first training session. T / F

C. Complete these sentences.

1. On Madison's jersey was the number _______________.
2. Some girls had played in the team for three or four _______________.
3. Two nice girls spoke to Madison – Bella and _______________.
4. Madison didn't believe the stories about the jersey. She said that anyone could have bad _______________.

D. Write short answers to these questions.

1. Who was the coach of Madison's new team?

   ____

2. What was the name of Madison's old team?

   ____

3. Who was the coach's daughter?

   ____

4. 'It's hard to join a new team in the middle of the year.' Who said this?

   ____

LANGUAGE ACTIVITIES

A. Write the correct prepositions in the spaces.

from next to at around

1. The girl _______________ Madison smiled.
2. The girls in the team stood _______________ the coach.
3. Things disappeared _______________ a girl's locker.
4. Daniel smiled _______________ Madison.

B. Write the past tense of these verbs.

1. come _______________ 3. throw _______________
2. think _______________ 4. feel _______________

WHAT DO YOU THINK?

Do you think that Madison's new jersey is going to be unlucky for her? Why or why not? Why do you think this?

____

Chapters 2 and 3

Before you read

A. Look at the picture on page 13 and circle the correct answers.

1. Who is Madison talking to?
   a. her coach b. her brother c. her friend
2. How do you think the coach feels towards Madison?
   a. He's pleased with her. b. He isn't happy with her.
   c. He thinks she's funny.

B. Find these words in your dictionary. Use them in the sentences.

wondered superstition curious newspaper

1. A lot of people believe the ______________ that breaking a mirror brings you bad luck for seven years.
2. Lara likes to read the ______________ on her way to work each day.
3. Ron ______________ how many stars were in the sky.
4. I'm ______________ to know what's in the big parcel from my grandparents.

C. Listen to Track 4 on the CD and answer these questions.

1. How did Madison feel when she went into the coach's office?
   a. happy b. nervous
2. What year did the log books go back to?
   a. 1975 b. 1970
3. Where did Madison see photographs of all the teams?
   a. on the bookshelf b. on the walls

After you read

Comprehension

A. Circle the correct answers.

1. When did the team start?
   a. more than twenty years ago b. more than thirty years ago
   c. more than forty years ago
2. How many weeks did the coach give Madison to start playing better?
   a. two weeks b. three weeks c. four weeks
3. What did Daniel use to eat the cake with?
   a. a knife b. a fork c. a spoon
4. How did Madison feel about the girl who disappeared in 1979?
   a. She was angry. b. She was happy. c. She was curious.

B. Circle T for true or F for false for these sentences.

1. Christine said Eva was nasty to everyone. T / F
2. Madison spoke to the coach in the changing room. T / F
3. Daniel went to the training session to play basketball. T / F
4. Madison took a large piece of cake from a box. T / F

C. Complete these sentences.

1. Madison felt the team lost because she played ______________.
2. Madison wasn't in the Jets now; she was in a new ______________.
3. The coach stared at a team photo on the wall – the one from ______________.
4. Daniel went to the training session on Monday ______________.

D. Write short answers to these questions.

1. What team was Madison going to play in if she didn't play better?
____
2. 'Loser!' Who said that to Madison?
____
3. Who went into the coach's office to find out the name of the girl who disappeared in 1979?
____
4. What was the name of the girl who disappeared in 1979?
____

Language activities

A. Match each word with its opposite from Chapters 2 and 3.

1. won	a. sad
2. bad	b. lost
3. happy	c. old
4. new	d. good

B. Write the missing vowels to make adverbs from Chapters 2 and 3.

1. k _ ndly	3. _ ngr _ ly
2. q _ _ _ tly	4. sl _ wly

What do you think?

Do you think that Madison and Daniel will find the girl who disappeared all those years ago? Why or why not?

____

Chapter 4

Before you read

A. Look at the picture on page 23 and circle the correct answers.

1. Who is talking on the phone?
   a. Madison b. Daniel c. the coach
2. What does Daniel have in his right hand?
   a. a pencil b. a book c. a phone

B. Find these words in your dictionary. Use them in the sentences.

phone book project whisper spooky

1. John tried to scare his sister by making some _______________ noises.
2. I don't want anyone else to hear this, so I'm going to _______________ in your ear.
3. Hamish looked up his friend's phone number in the _______________.
4. Liam has to finish a big school _______________ by Friday.

C. Listen to Track 5 on the CD and answer these questions.

1. When did Madison and Daniel go to the library?
   a. on Tuesday b. on Thursday
2. What did they go onto after they got home?
   a. the radio b. the Internet
3. Where did Daniel say they could find the Lucases from Colby?
   a. in the phone book b. at basketball practice

After you read

Comprehension

A. Circle the correct answers.

1. How many people with the name of Lucas were there in Colby?
   a. about twenty b. about thirty c. about forty
2. When was Madison's big game going to be?
   a. on Friday b. on Saturday c. on Sunday
3. Which number did Daniel say was 'spooky'?
   a. number seven b. number eight c. number nine
4. What did Madison throw at Daniel's head?
   a. a cushion b. a basketball c. the phone

B. Circle T for true or F for false for these sentences.

1. Madison called the first person on the list. T / F
2. Daniel spoke to Maxine Lucas's second cousin. T / F
3. Madison was nervous about her big game. T / F
4. Maxine Lucas still lived in the town of Colby. T / F

C. Complete these sentences.

1. Madison didn't know what to say. She wanted Daniel to do the ______________.
2. Daniel told people he was doing a history ______________.
3. Daniel held his thumb up to his ______________.
4. When Mr Lucas called back, Madison and Daniel were in the ______________.

D. Write short answers to these questions.

1. How many people with the name of Lucas did Madison and Daniel call?
   ____
2. When did Mr Lucas call Daniel back?
   ____
3. Who was going to meet Madison and Daniel at Mimo's Café?
   ____
4. Where was Mimo's Café?
   ____

Language activities

A. Circle the correct verb forms in these sentences.

1. Daniel **was** / **were** already at the library.
2. The library didn't **has** / **have** newspapers from 1979.
3. Daniel sat down and **find** / **found** the right page.
4. Daniel looked at Madison and **shake** / **shook** his head.

B. Write the missing vowels to make nouns from Chapter 4.

1. d _ ys
2. m _ n _ t _ s
3. y _ _ rs
4. t _ m _ s

What do you think?

Do you think that Madison and Daniel will find out what happened to Maxine Lucas all those years ago? Why or why not?

____

Chapters 5 and 6

Before you read

A. Look at the picture on page 28 and circle the correct answers.

1. Where are Madison and Daniel?
   a. at home b. at the library c. in a café
2. What is on the table?
   a. a cup b. a newspaper c. a photograph

B. Find these words in your dictionary. Use them in the sentences.

whistle divorce bullying horrible

1. Since his parents' ______________, Joe only sees his father on Sundays.
2. Martin can't cook. The cake he made tasted ______________.
3. Colin was very unhappy. Some nasty boys were ______________ him at school.
4. The guard blew his ______________ and the train started moving.

C. Listen to Track 6 on the CD and answer these questions.

1. Why did Maxine run away from home?
   a. Because she was unhappy. b. Because she wanted to have fun.
2. Where did she sleep after she ran away from home?
   a. in a warm bed b. down by the river
3. How long did she live there?
   a. for three weeks b. for three months

After you read

COMPREHENSION

A. Circle the correct answers.

1. What did Madison and Daniel order at the café?
   a. hot coffees b. hot chocolates c. iced chocolates
2. What number jersey did Maxine Lucas wear when she played basketball?
   a. number seven b. number eight c. number nine
3. How did it feel when Madison stood up to Eva on the basketball court?
   a. good b. spooky c. strange
4. Who gave Maxine's note to Madison?
   a. Eva b. the coach c. Christine

B. Circle T for true or F for false for these sentences.

1. Maxine used to play for the Colby Raiders. T / F
2. Maxine's mother moved out of Colby. T / F
3. The coach wrote Madison a note. T / F
4. Madison's parents came to the basketball game. T / F

C. Complete these sentences.

1. Madison and Daniel wanted to ask Maxine some ______________.
2. Maxine and her mother started a new ______________.
3. On Saturday morning Madison felt ______________.
4. On the court, Madison looked down and touched her ______________.

D. Write short answers to these questions.

1. What was the name of the nasty girl in the team when Maxine played basketball?

   ____

2. 'You play your best and be sure to stand up to Eva.' Who said this to Madison?

   ____

3. Who did Maxine go and sit next to at the basketball game?

   ____

4. What did Madison think was going to be lucky for her?

   ____

LANGUAGE ACTIVITIES

A. Write the correct prepositions in the spaces.

under from near outside

1. Madison and Daniel stood ______________ the café before going in.
2. Maxine ran away ______________ home.
3. Daniel went to a table ______________ the front of the café and picked up a newspaper.
4. Maxine looked at the names ______________ the picture.

B. Write the missing vowels to make verbs from Chapters 5 and 6.

1. _ nd _ rst _ nd
2. r _ m _ mb _ r
3. kn _ w
4. th _ nk

WHAT DO YOU THINK?

Madison stood up to Eva. Who did Maxine Lucas stand up to? How did this help Maxine?

____

Glossary

adj. adjective; *adv.* adverb; *n.* noun; *pron.* pronoun; *v.* verb

accident /ˈæksɪd(ə)nt/ *n.*	Unfall
alone /əˈləʊn/ *adj.*	einsam
around /əˈraʊnd/ *adv.*	herum
basketball /ˈbɑːskɪtˌbɔːl/ *n.*	Basketball
blow /bləʊ/ *v.*	pfeifen, ertönen
bookshelf /ˈbʊkˌʃelf/ *n.*	Bücherregal
bother /ˈbɒðə/ *v.*	belästigen
bounce /baʊns/ *v.*	hüpfen
breath /breθ/ *n.*	*hier:* Luft
bully /ˈbʊli/ *v.*	tyrannisieren, schikanieren
calm /kɑːm/ *adj.*	ruhig
changing room /ˈtʃeɪndʒɪŋ ˌruːm/ *n.*	Umkleidekabine
coach /kəʊtʃ/ *n.*	Trainer, -in
court /kɔːt/ *n.*	Spielfeld
curious /ˈkjʊəriəs/ *adj.*	neugierig
cushion /ˈkʊʃn/ *n.*	Kissen
decide /dɪˈsaɪd/ *v.*	entscheiden
disappear /ˌdɪsəˈpɪə/ *v.*	verschwinden
divorce /dɪˈvɔːs/ *n.*	Scheidung
dug /dʌg/ *v.*	*hier:* stoßen (*past tense* von *dig*)
else /els/ *adv.*	anderes
feel /fiːl/ *v.*	fühlen
fight /faɪt/ *n.*	Schlägerei
gate /geɪt/ *n.*	Tor
give up /gɪv ʌp/ *v.*	aufhören
glare /gleə/ *v.*	starren, anstarren
gossip /ˈgɒsɪp/ *n.*	Klatsch, Tratsch, Gerede
groan /grəʊn/ *v.*	stöhnen

hoop /huːp/ *n.*	Korb (*beim Basketball*)
horrible /ˈhɒrəbl/ *adj.*	schrecklich
hug /hʌg/ *n.*	Umarmung
jersey /ˈdʒɜːzi/ *n.*	Trikot
join /dʒɔɪn/ *v.*	anschließen
kidnap /ˈkɪdnæp/ *v.*	entführen
kill /kɪl/ *v.*	töten
last /lɑːst/ *adj.*	letzte/r/s
adv.	zuletzt
library /ˈlaɪbrəri/ *n.*	Bibliothek
log book /lɒg bʊk/ *n.*	Mannschaftsbuch, Teambuch
look forward to /lʊk ˈfɔːwəd tʊ/ *v.*	sich auf etwas freuen
lose /luːz/ *v.*	verlieren
luck /lʌk/ *n.*	Glück
magic /ˈmædʒɪk/ *n.*	Zauberei
murder /ˈmɜːdə/ *n.*	Mord
nervous /ˈnɜːvəs/ *adj.*	nervös
newspaper /ˈnjuːzˌpeɪpə/ *n.*	Zeitung
no one /ˈnəʊ ˌwʌn/ *pron.*	niemand
nod /nɒd/ *v.*	nicken
note /nəʊt/ *n.*	Notiz
of course /ˈəv ˌkɔːs/ *adv.*	natürlich
office /ˈɒfɪs/ *n.*	Büro
order /ˈɔːdə/ *v.*	bestellen
phone book /ˈfəʊn ˌbʊk/ *n.*	Telefonbuch
pick up /ˌpɪk ˈʌp/ *v.*	*hier:* nehmen
project /ˈprɒdʒekt/ *n.*	Projekt
push open /pʊʃ ˈəʊpən/ *v.*	aufstoßen
scare /skeə/ *v.*	Angst machen (*to be scared* – Angst haben)
shelf /ʃelf/ *n.*	Regal
shook /ʃuːk/ *v.*	schütteln (*past tense* von *shake*)
shrug /ʃrʌg/ *v.*	zucken
sigh /saɪ/ *v.*	seufzen

spooky /ˈspuːki/ *adj.*	unheimlich
stand up to /stænd ʌp tʊ/ *v.*	sich durchsetzen, sich behaupten gegenüber
stomach /ˈstʌmək/ *n.*	Magen
suddenly /ˈsʌdnli/ *adv.*	plötzlich
superstition /ˌsuːpəˈstɪʃn/ *n.*	Aberglaube
superstitious /ˌsuːpəˈstɪʃes/ *adj.*	abergläubisch
sure /ʃʊə/ *adj.*	sicher
team /tiːm/ *n.*	Mannschaft
teammate /ˈtiːmˌmeɪt/ *n.*	Mitspieler, -in
threw /θruː/ *v.*	werfen (*past tense* von *throw*)
toast /təʊst/ *n.*	Toast
together /təˈgeðə/ *adv.*	zusammen
training session /ˈtreɪnɪŋ ˌseʃn/ *n.*	Training
trouble /ˈtrʌbl/ *n.*	Ärger
true /truː/ *adj.*	wahr
turn /tɜːn/ *v.*	sich umdrehen
upset /ʌpˈset/ *v.*	aufregen, verärgern
used to /ˈjuːst tuː/ *v.*	früher
usually /ˈjuːʒʊəli/ *adv.*	gewöhnlich
wave /weɪv/ *v.*	winken, zuwinken
way /weɪ/ *n.*	Weise
what kind of /wɒt kaɪnd əv/	was für
whisper /ˈwɪspə/ *v.*	flüstern
whistle /ˈwɪsl/ *n.*	Pfiff
wonder /ˈwʌndə/ *v.*	sich fragen
worry /ˈwʌri/ *v.*	sich Sorgen machen

Lucky for Some
Activities: Answer Key

Chapter 1

Before you read

A. 1. b, 2. a B. 1. disappeared, 2. usually, 3. join, 4. toast C. 1. a, 2. a, 3. b

After you read

Comprehension

A. 1. b, 2. a, 3. b, 4. c B. 1. T, 2. F, 3. T, 4. F C. 1. nine, 2. years, 3. Christine, 4. luck D. 1. Mr Roberts, 2. Jesmond Jets, 3. Eva, 4. Bella

Language activities

A. 1. next to, 2. around, 3. from, 4. at
B. 1. came, 2. thought, 3. threw, 4. felt

What do you think?

Students' own answers

Chapters 2 and 3

Before you read

A. 1. a, 2. b B. 1. superstition, 2. newspaper, 3. wondered, 4. curious
C. 1. b, 2. a, 3. b

After you read

Comprehension

A. 1. b, 2. a, 3. b, 4. c B. 1. T, 2. F, 3. F, 4. T C. 1. badly, 2. team, 3. 1979, 4. afternoon D. 1. the B Team, 2. Eva, 3. Daniel, 4. Maxine Lucas

Language activities

A. 1. b, 2. d, 3. a, 4. c B. 1. kindly, 2. quietly, 3. angrily, 4. slowly

What do you think?

Students' own answers

Chapter 4

Before you read

A. 1. b, 2. a B. 1. spooky, 2. whisper, 3. phone book, 4. project C. 1. a, 2. b, 3. a

After you read

Comprehension

A. 1. b, 2. b, 3. c, 4. a B. 1. F, 2. T, 3. T, 4. F C. 1. talking, 2. project, 3. sister, 4. kitchen D. 1. nine, 2. on Friday evening, 3. Maxine Lucas, 4. in the Mall

Language activities

A. 1. was, 2. have, 3. found, 4. shook
B. 1. days, 2. minutes, 3. years, 4. times

What do you think?

Students' own answers

Chapters 5 and 6

Before you read

A. 1. c, 2. a B. 1. divorce, 2. horrible, 3. bullying, 4. whistle C. 1. a, 2. b, 3. b

After you read

Comprehension

A. 1. b, 2. c, 3. a, 4. b B. 1. T, 2. T, 3. F, 4. T C. 1. questions, 2. life, 3. sick, 4. jersey D. 1. Anita, 2. Maxine, 3. Daniel, 4. number nine

Language activities

A. 1. outside, 2. from, 3. near, 4. under
B. 1. understand, 2. remember, 3. know, 4. think

What do you think?

Students' own answers